A Note to Parents and Teachers

Eyewitness Readers is a compelling new reading programme for children. *Eyewitness* has become the most trusted name in illustrated books and this new series combines the highly visual *Eyewitness* approach with engaging, easy-to-read stories. Each *Eyewitness Reader* is guaranteed to capture a child's interest while developing his or her reading skills, general knowledge and love of reading.

The books are written by leading children's authors and are designed in conjunction with literacy experts, including Cliff Moon M.Ed., Honorary Fellow of the University of Reading. Cliff Moon spent many years as a teacher and teacher educator specializing in reading. He has written more than 140 books for children and teachers and he reviews regularly for teachers' journals.

The four levels of *Eyewitness Readers* are aimed at different reading abilities, enabling you to choose the books that are exactly right for each child.

Level One – Beginning to read
Level Two – Beginning to read alone
Level Three – Reading alone
Level Four – Proficient readers

The "normal" age at which a child begins to read can be anywhere from three to eight years old, so these levels are intended only as a general guideline.

No matter which level you select, you can be sure that you're helping children learn to read, then read to learn!

Launch
OF
White Star Royal Mail Triple-Screw Steamer
"TITANIC"
At BELFAST,
Wednesday, 31st May, 1911, at 12.15 p.m.
Admit Bearer:

A Dorling Kindersley Book
www.dk.com

Project Editor Shaila Awan
Designer Michelle Baxter
Senior Editor Linda Esposito
Managing Art Editor Peter Bailey
Production Josie Alabaster
Picture Researcher Louise Thomas
Illustrator Peter Dennis

Titanic Consultant
Eric Kentley Ph.D.

Reading Consultant
Cliff Moon M.Ed.

Published in Great Britain by Dorling Kindersley Limited
9 Henrietta Street, London WC2E 8PS

6 8 10 9 7 5

Eyewitness Readers™ is a trademark of
Dorling Kindersley Ltd.

A CIP catalogue record for this book is
available from the British Library.

ISBN 0-7513-5860-6

Colour reproduction by Colourscan, Singapore
Printed and bound in Belgium by Proost

The publisher would like to thank Jules Verne Aventures and the
following for their kind permission to reproduce their photographs:
Key: a=above, t=top, b=below, l=left, r=right, c=centre

Brown Brothers: 37; Colorific: ©P. Landmann/Arenok 43br, ©RMS
Titanic/Arenok 42t; Corbis: Library of Congress 4br, Ralph White
41tr; Corbis-Bettmann: 34br, 34bc, Underwood & Underwood 7tr;
Mary Evans Picture Library: 33b, 35tr; John Frost Historical
Newspapers: 35bl; Hulton Getty: 6cl, 20, 21br; The Irish Picture
Library: Fr. Browne S.J. Collection 35cr; The Library of Congress,
Washington: 38t; Walter Lord Collection: 31tr; Don Lynch
Collection: 8br; MacQuitty International Photo Collection: 19br;
The Board of Trustees of the National Museums & Galleries on
Merseyside: 7br; Reproduced by the kind permission of Elisabeth
Navratil: 47c; Rex Features: 35tl, Sachs 2br, 5b; Southampton City
Cultural Services: 36br; Sygma: ©Ocean Research and Expedition
43bla, 44br, A. Tannenbaum 40bl; Ulster Folk and Transport
Museum: TR59/4 1br, Harland & Wolff Collection H1455 41br.

Jacket: **Ronald Grant**: front; **Rex Features**:
Nils Jorgansen back tl, back tr.

Contents

EYEWITNESS ● READERS

READING
3
ALONE

TITANIC

THE DISASTER THAT SHOCKED THE WORLD!

Written by Mark Dubowski

DK

DORLING KINDERSLEY
London • New York • Sydney
www.dk.com

The greatest ship

When the White Star Line announced the completion of the "supership" – the *Titanic* – in 1912, they said that she was the greatest ship ever built: luxurious, unsinkable and unbelievably big.

How big was she? The *Titanic* was more than 269 metres (882 feet) long. That's the length of 22 buses lined up end to end. She was the largest movable object in the world. When the *Titanic* passed a small ship, she was like a cloud going by. A big, black cloud that blotted out the sun.

Gigantic propellers
Everything about the *Titanic* was big. Each of her three propellers was as big as a windmill.

The *Titanic*'s hull, or lower body, was divided into sixteen compartments. Up to four could flood and she would still be able to float.

The *Titanic* was like a floating palace with elegant restaurants, Turkish baths and a swimming pool. There were separate rooms, lounges and eating areas for first, second and third class.

Reading and writing room

Gymnasium

First-class lounge

Private promenade

Third-class dining room

Sauna and steam room

The section of the Titanic *illustrated below*
is shown in this box.

Wooden
lifeboat

Funnel

First-class
suite
rooms

Grand
staircase

First-class
staterooms

Turkish baths   Swimming pool   Third-class cabins

7

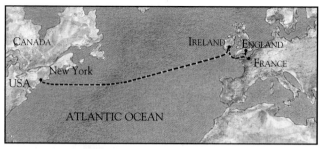

On her route, the Titanic *would also dock in France and Ireland to pick up passengers.*

On her maiden voyage the *Titanic* would sail across the Atlantic, from England to New York in the USA.

In charge of the *Titanic* was Captain

Captain Edward J. Smith

Edward J. Smith. He would navigate from the bridge at the front of the ship. This was to be his last voyage before retiring.

Newspapers called the ship "the Millionaires' Special" but its passengers were really from all walks of life.

John Jacob Astor and his wife had first-class tickets. They were among the wealthiest passengers and had a suite, or group of rooms, fit for a king.

Not-so-rich people were going, too. Many were emigrants – with all their possessions in their luggage – hoping to start a new life in America.

Colonel John Jacob Astor and his wife, Madeleine.

A costly ticket!
A first-class ticket for the *Titanic* cost more than a crew member could earn in 18 years!

All aboard!

At last the *Titanic* is ready to set sail from England, teeming with more than a thousand passengers. Among them are dozens of children. Edmond and Michel Navratil from France are travelling in second class with their father. They are only two and three years old.

Crowds on the dock are waving flags and handkerchiefs. Some are cheering, while others are shouting, "Good luck, *Titanic*!" Passengers are waving good-bye to friends and family.

Kennel class

Some passengers took their dogs, which were kept in kennels and exercised every day. The Astors took their Airedale, named Kitty.

Danger ahead!

13 April
After three days at sea, the trip has seemed like a holiday for most of the passengers. But soon, the *Titanic* will be entering an area of the north Atlantic Ocean where icebergs float.

14 April 11:40 P.M.
All day the *Titanic* has received iceberg warnings in Morse code over the wireless. Now, as the ship speeds through the night, two lookouts watch for icebergs from the crow's nest.

All is quiet on this freezing-cold night and the ocean is incredibly calm.

Mighty icebergs

Icebergs are big pieces of floating ice. They are a danger to ships because most of an iceberg is hidden under the water.

But then, with their watch about to come to an end, the lookouts see a dark object looming ahead. It is an iceberg . . . and the *Titanic* is heading straight towards it!

Quickly one of the lookouts sounds the alarm bell and shouts into the telephone connected to the bridge, "Iceberg right ahead!"

With no time to waste, the First Officer calls for the ship's wheel to be turned as far as possible. Then he orders the engines to be stopped and put into reverse.

High in the crow's nest, the lookouts brace themselves for a collision as the

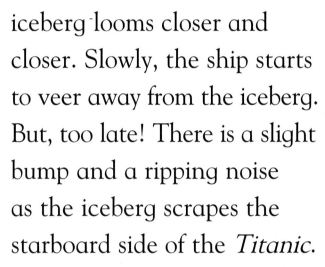

iceberg looms closer and closer. Slowly, the ship starts to veer away from the iceberg. But, too late! There is a slight bump and a ripping noise as the iceberg scrapes the starboard side of the *Titanic*.

Many passengers are asleep. The small bump to the ship isn't enough to disturb them. But it wakes up Captain Smith. He rushes to the bridge to find out what has happened.

Down below, the men working in one of the boiler rooms are almost swept off their feet as water gushes into the room. Within minutes the water is waist-high.

Automatic doors begin to seal the flooding compartments. The men rush to escape before the doors shut. But the water is rising higher and higher and flowing over the tops of the compartments, flooding one after another.

15 April 12:05 A.M. "Uncover the boats!" Captain Smith orders his crew. Then he instructs the two wireless operators to start signalling for help. He knows the *Titanic* is going to sink – and he knows that there are not enough lifeboats to get all the passengers off safely.

17

Not far from the panic in the boiler rooms, many passengers are still fast asleep, unaware of the collision.

Out on the third-class deck, a few passengers find chunks of ice and start playing football. They have no idea how much danger they are in.

Very soon all the passengers are ordered on deck with their life jackets on. Many come up from their rooms in their night clothes but some are still wearing their evening dress.

Colonel Astor and his wife make their way to the gymnasium next to the boat deck. While they wait for the crew to get a lifeboat ready, Colonel Astor cuts through a spare life jacket to show his wife what is inside.

Now the crew begins to direct the passengers into the boats. "Women and children first!" they shout.

Life jackets

Inside a life jacket were several floats about the size of a paperback book. This helped to keep the wearer afloat. The *Titanic* had enough life jackets for all the passengers.

Lifeboats are slowly lowered into the ocean by ropes, which pass through the pulleys on cranes, called davits.

15 April 12:45 A.M. The crew lowers the first lifeboat 60 feet (18 metres) down to the ocean. But there are only 28 people in a boat for 65. The passengers don't want to leave the *Titanic*. The lifeboats seem unsteady compared to the big ship. The band is even playing cheerful music.

One by one the lifeboats are lowered, when disaster looms. Boat number 13 drifts under another lifeboat that is being lowered. The boat nearly crashes on top of number 13. At the last moment, a passenger frees the ropes holding number 13 and the boat floats away to safety.

Lifeboats

The *Titanic* had 20 lifeboats. The davits could have held an extra 16 lifeboats but the owners did not want the decks to look crowded.

As the lifeboats are lowered, lights are seen on the horizon – another ship is out there! It is far away but the *Titanic*'s crew members have a way to get its attention. They fire distress rockets that explode like fireworks in the sky. Then they use the Morse lamp. But there is no response.

The *Titanic*'s wireless operators keep calling for help. Although other ships are close enough, the wireless operators on some of these ships are asleep.

The *Olympic*, the *Titanic*'s sister ship, has heard the distress call. But she is too far away to be able to help.

15 April 1:15 A.M. Slowly, slowly, the bow sinks farther down. Slowly, slowly, the stern rises above it.

The band plays on, trying to keep the passengers calm. But now there is fear – the passengers realize that the *Titanic* is sinking.

15 April 2:05 A.M. The last wooden lifeboat is about to be lowered. Colonel Astor is waving good-bye to his wife. He is not allowed to board. With more than 1,500 passengers still left, the crew has formed a protective circle around the lifeboat so that only women and children can take the last few seats.

Colonel Astor rushes to the kennels, where his dog Kitty is kept. He sets all the dogs free so they will not be trapped.

Michel and Edmond Navratil are still on the ship. Their father has wrapped them in blankets to keep them warm. Their only hope of escape is in the last collapsible boat about to be launched. Their father pushes forward and hands them to a woman sitting in the boat. Then he steps back into the crowd.

The music has stopped now but the ship's lights are still glowing in the dark. As the stern rises higher into the air, everything inside the ship slides to the front. Furniture, statues, paintings, dishes, luggage – every object on board crashes down and piles up.

Out on the deck there are still hundreds of passengers. The slant on the deck is so steep now that they cannot stand up straight. Some are clinging desperately to the rails. Others lose their grip and fall into the sea. It is a long drop, like a fall from a tall building.

Those wearing life jackets are kept afloat. But the water is ice-cold and they will soon freeze to death if they are not rescued.

15 April 2:20 A.M. The *Titanic*'s lights flicker as she plunges . . . then she's gone. People in the water scream for help but their cries soon die down. The survivors huddle together, cold and afraid.

Here in the north Atlantic, there is no first, second or third class. Rich and poor, young and old – they are all in this together now. All of them hoping to survive, none of them knowing what will happen next.

The survivors in the lifeboats had rowed away from the ship, fearing that they would either be sucked down with the *Titanic* as she sank or be swamped by the people in the water.

But now some sailors decide to row back to the floating wreckage of the *Titanic*.

They want to see if anyone is still alive.
They row through hundreds of frozen
bodies and find just four survivors.
One dies shortly after he is pulled into
the boat.

The rescue

15 April 3:30 A.M.

It is almost dawn. The survivors have been at sea for several hours now, without food, water or warm clothing. Many are almost frozen to death. Suddenly, they see rockets in the distance. Another ship is on its way – help has arrived!

It is the *Carpathia*. Her crew had heard the *Titanic*'s distress calls. But the ship was 93 kilometres (58 miles) away – a three-hour trip. She has arrived too late to save the people in the water but not too late to save the people in the lifeboats.

A race against time

After receiving the distress message, the *Carpathia* raced through the dangerous icefields. She was the first ship to arrive at the scene.

One by one, the *Titanic* survivors board the *Carpathia*. Some climb a rope ladder to reach the deck of the ship. Others who are too weak or too young to climb are hauled aboard in cargo nets. Everyone is counted: of the 2,206 passengers, only 705 people have survived.

The *Carpathia* now heads for New York. The journey will take three days.

The dazed survivors are given warm clothes and food.

18 April Friends and relatives have been frantic for news. They are confused by the different reports. The *Carpathia* is not releasing any information and newspapers are making up stories. One says everyone survived and that the *Titanic* is being towed by another ship. Other newspapers say many have died.

In New York, people wait anxiously for the *Carpathia*, hoping they will see their loved ones step off the ship.

People start to gather along the pier at New York harbour.

Newspapers are filled with conflicting stories of the disaster.

18 April 9:25 P.M. At last the *Carpathia* sails into New York harbour. Nearly 30,000 people are lining the dock. Among them are many doctors and nurses sent to help the survivors.

The gangplank is lowered from the *Carpathia* and the first survivors walk down. People on the dock rush forward. Some call out the names of their relatives.

Harold Bride, the only surviving wireless operator, is carried off the ship. His feet are badly frostbitten and have been bandaged. Also among the survivors are two dogs.

Heroes of the disaster

The grateful survivors of the *Titanic* disaster presented this medal to the crew of the *Carpathia* for saving their lives.

Harold Bride was washed overboard as the Titanic *sank. He managed to climb on to an overturned lifeboat.*

Michel and Edmond Navratil with their mother

Michel and Edmond Navratil are safe. A survivor is looking after them until they can be reunited with their mother, Marcelle, in France. She did not know that they were on the *Titanic*.

The children's father had been separated from their mother and had kidnapped the boys. He had told travellers that their mother was dead. Marcelle recognized her sons from a photograph in a French newspaper, telling the tragic story about the two "orphaned" boys.

Mrs. Astor is among the survivors. She had helped to row her lifeboat away from the sinking *Titanic*.

Out in the ocean, ships are finding bodies of the victims. Many of them cannot be identified. But Colonel Astor's body is identified. His initials are printed on his shirt collar.

Captain Smith's body is not found among the 328 bodies recovered. Some reports say that he was standing on the bridge before the ship sank.

Discovered

In the years after the *Titanic* sank, many people wanted to find her. But the ship's exact location was a mystery and the technology didn't exist to reach her even if her whereabouts had been known. The *Titanic* had plunged 3,798 metres (12,460 feet) – that's the height of 39 Big Ben clock towers!

Dr. Robert Ballard was the scientist in charge of the expedition.

More than 70 years passed. Then in 1985 a team led by Dr. Robert Ballard used an unmanned diving vessel called *Argo*, which had a video camera that sent pictures back to the research ship.

The explorers sent *Argo* down to the bottom of the ocean. Day after day they searched the seabed for signs of the wreck but saw nothing.

This is an image of the front of a boiler, which was found lying on the Atlantic seabed.

Then, one day, an object appeared on the monitor of the research ship – it was an image of a huge boiler. The *Titanic* had been found! She had broken into two and her contents were spilled across the seabed.

The Titanic *had 29 boilers. The picture above shows the boilers before they were installed on the* Titanic.

The Nautile, *a small submersible, was carried by a special research ship to the site of the wreck and then launched.*

Two years later, another submersible, the *Nautile*, visited the *Titanic*. It was equipped with the latest technology, including a movable video camera that could film inside the rooms of the *Titanic*.

The *Nautile* also had two robotic arms, which were operated by a pilot inside the submersible. These arms had different attachments that enabled the pilot to pick up various types of objects.

The *Nautile* brought back thousands of ordinary objects that were scattered over the seabed: toys, eyeglasses, money and jewels. They were small but sad reminders of the many lost lives.

Once on dry land, the objects were carefully cleaned and restored so that they could be displayed in exhibitions. These objects helped to tell the story of the *Titanic* and her passengers.

Nautile's robotic arm is used to pick up this safe. Part of the safe had rotted away and it was empty.

This money was also retrieved by the Nautile. *It was found inside a bag that was lying on the seabed.*

Nautile's technology also enabled scientists to answer a question that had remained a mystery since the sinking: What really did happen to the *Titanic*?

Nautile's evidence showed that the iceberg did not carve a 91-metre (300-foot) gash along the side of the *Titanic* as suspected. Instead, the iceberg had made six small cuts below the waterline, which had allowed the water to gush into her hull.

By examining the wreck of the *Titanic*, scientists were also able to explain exactly how she broke apart.

Deep diver

Nautile can carry three people. It is one of only six submersibles in the world that can dive deep enough to reach the wreck.

How the *Titanic* sank

1. The *Titanic* hits the iceberg, which scrapes the ship in six places. Water gushes in through the narrow openings.

2. The compartments flood, one after another. The weight of the water in the bow starts to pull the ship under.

3. The front funnel collapses. Then, as the stern rises into the air, the other funnels also start to crash under the strain.

4. The strain on the ship is so great that she breaks apart. The bow plunges to the bottom. The stern starts to flood and then sinks.

Lessons of the *Titanic*

When the *Titanic* sank in 1912 a full inquiry was launched at the time. Many questions were asked: Would the *Titanic* have sunk if she had not sailed at full speed on that fatal night? Was her design at fault?

All these issues were discussed. But more importantly, new safety regulations for passenger liners were passed.

Ships had to carry enough lifeboats for everyone. Wireless operators had to listen to their radios all night long. A special airborne Ice Patrol was set up to help warn ships of dangerous icebergs.

Never again would people dare call any ship "unsinkable". The *Titanic* was a cruel lesson for everyone.

Michel Navratil talks to another survivor at a Titanic *reunion in 1995. He could recall being placed in a sack and then hauled to safety on board the* Carpathia.

Glossary

Boiler
A furnace that boils water to create steam. This powers the ship.

Bow
The front part of a ship.

Bridge
An area at the front of a ship from which it is steered.

Collapsible boat
A boat with canvas sides, which can be collapsed so that the boat can be stored easily.

Crow's nest
A platform on a ship's mast from which lookouts watch for danger.

Davits
Crane-like mechanisms used for holding or lowering lifeboats.

Dock
A place where ships arrive and depart.

Emigrants
People who move from one country to live in another.

First class
The highest level of comfort on a ship. People who go first class pay a higher fare than others.

Funnel
A pipe or chimney that enables smoke from the boiler room to escape.

Hull
A ship's body.

Lifeboat
A boat used by people if they have to abandon ship.

Maiden voyage
The first time a ship makes a journey in service.

Morse code
A system of dots and dashes for each letter of the alphabet.

Morse lamp
A lamp used to flash distress signals in Morse code.

Propellers
Shafts with blades. A ship's engines drive the propellers around and this pushes a ship forward.

Rocket
A small device that makes a bright light in the sky. Used as a distress signal.

Second class
A level of comfort that is not as expensive as first class and with fewer services.

Starboard
The right-hand side of a ship when facing the front of a ship.

Stern
The rear part of a ship.

Submersible
A boat that travels underwater.

Third class
The lowest level of comfort on a ship. People in third class pay the lowest fare and get very few services.

Wireless
A telegraph machine that sends messages by radio waves.